The Great Space Race

by
Rosalind Brown

Art Toby Mikle

www.rosalindbrownbooks.com

Artwork by Toby Mikle of MyBookIllustrator.com

For Elliot & Adam,

my shining stars.

- Rosalind

This Book Belongs To:

In the middle of our solar system
Far away in space,
Are eight excited aliens
Getting ready for a race.

The Sun is where they're starting
A long way past the Moon,
The finish line is Neptune
They'll blast off very soon.

The aliens rev their engines
They give their horns a blow,
It's getting a bit hot now
So it's 3,2,1 – let's go!

Whooshing through the galaxy
They soon reach Mercury,
This planet's busy whizzing
Round the Sun at lightning speed.

One alien gets distracted
He thinks this looks good fun,
So he chases after Mercury
To run rings around the Sun.

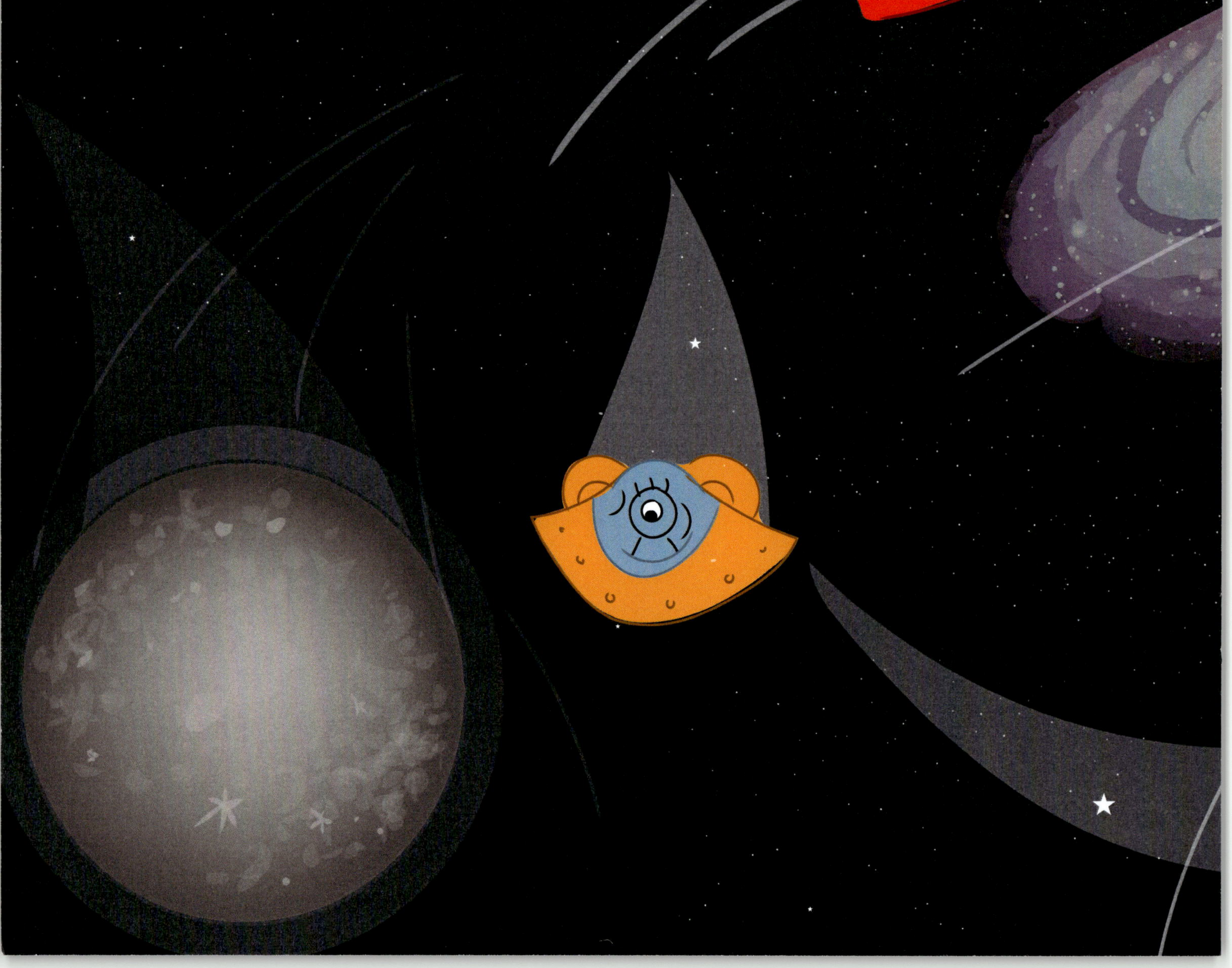

The other seven carry on
All keen to win first prize,
When Venus suddenly appears
With a fiery surprise.

Its blistering volcanoes
Spout hot lava in the air,
One vehicle gets a sizzling splash
Its driver gets a scare!

The six remaining aliens
Race ahead for all they're worth,
They see a ball of blue and green
Of course they've spotted Earth!

High above the swirling clouds
They pass a big space station,
One alien meets an astronaut
And stops for conversation.

The pace is picking up now
As five whizz beneath the stars,
A small red dot comes into view
They're fast approaching Mars.

It's really rather windy
On this planet full of dust,
'My windscreen!' cries one alien
It's covered with one gust.

Four aliens zooming onwards
They pass a meteor shower,
Up next is mighty Jupiter
Huge and full of power.

They fly above the Great Red Spot
A storm that howls and rages,
One alien gets sucked inside
He'll be blown around for ages!

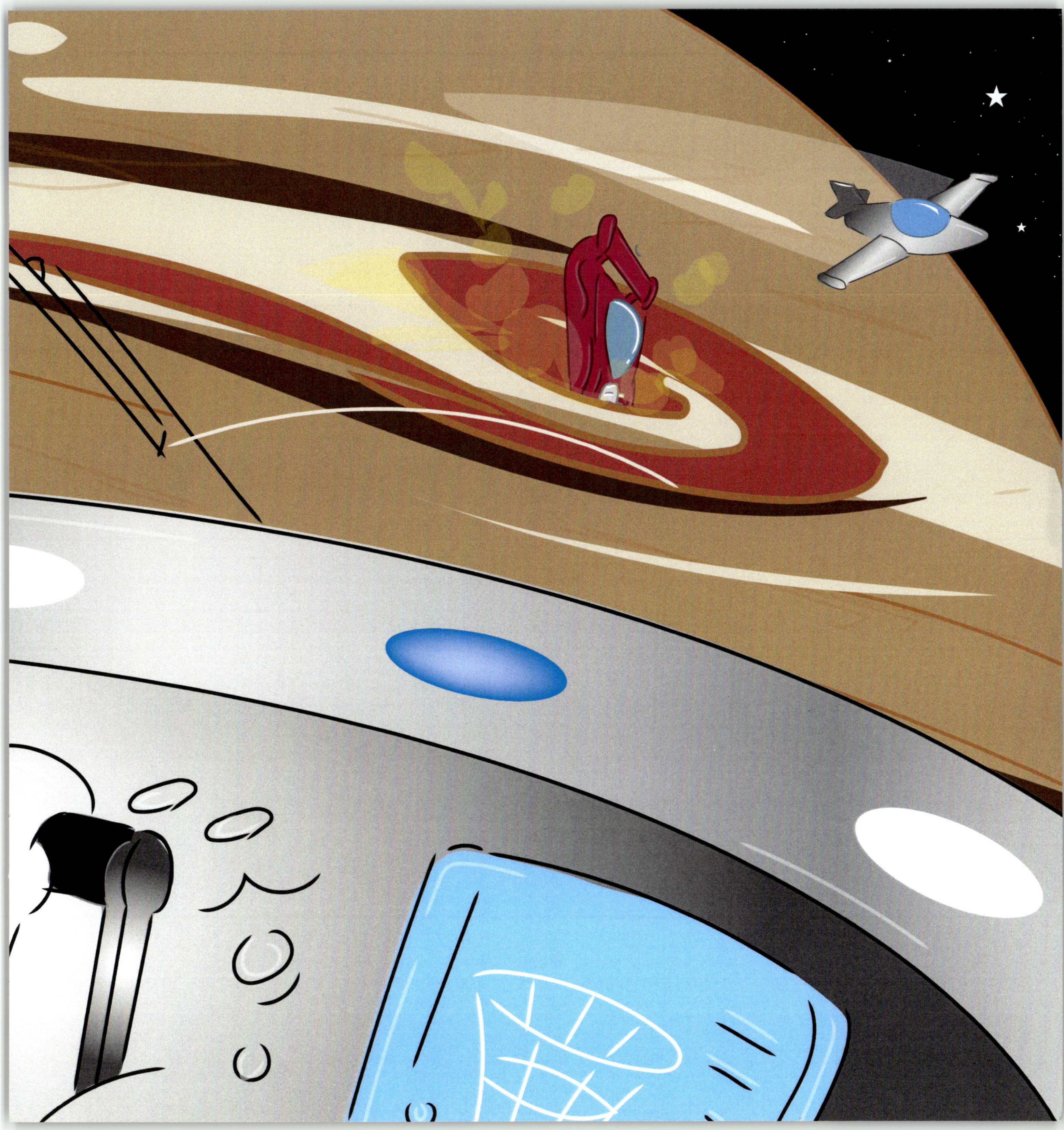

Just three competitors left now
All shouting with delight,
For floating there in front of them
Is a most impressive sight.

It's Saturn with its sparkly rings
Of glittering rock and ice,
One alien stops to stare at them
After all they do look nice.

The final two zip forwards
They're feeling such a thrill,
When Uranus appears (uh-oh!)
And sends an icy chill.

This planet's oh-so-freezing
As cold as it can get,
One vehicle loses power
There's ice inside the jets!

Just one alien hurtling
Towards Neptune big and blue,
She whooshes past the finish line
And shouts a loud 'Woohoo!'

FINISH

But now she feels quite lonely
And misses all her friends,
It's not much fun to win a race
When no-one's at the end.

But what's that distant cheering?
The others all appear!
It's time to fly back home now
And they'll race again next year.

Fun Facts about our Solar System!

The Sun is a star, a huge ball of very hot glowing gases. It's more than a million times bigger than the Earth.

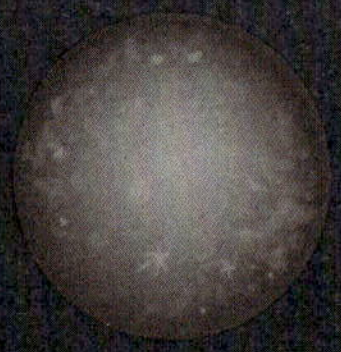

Mercury is the smallest planet. It's the closest planet to the Sun.

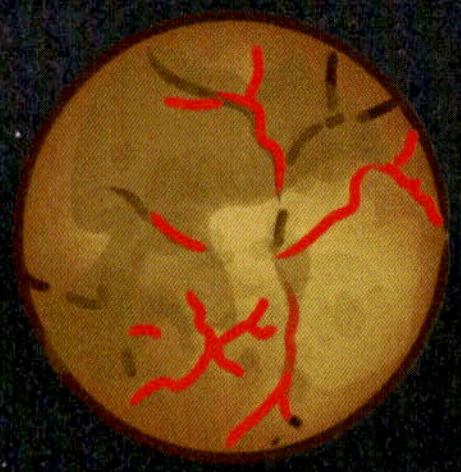

Venus is the hottest planet. It has thousands of volcanoes on its surface.

Earth is the planet we live on. Most of the Earth is covered in water.

Neptune is the furthest planet from the Sun. It takes 160 years to go round the Sun.

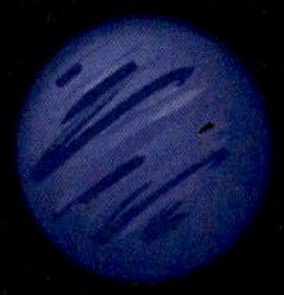

Uranus is the coldest planet. It's the only planet that spins on its side.

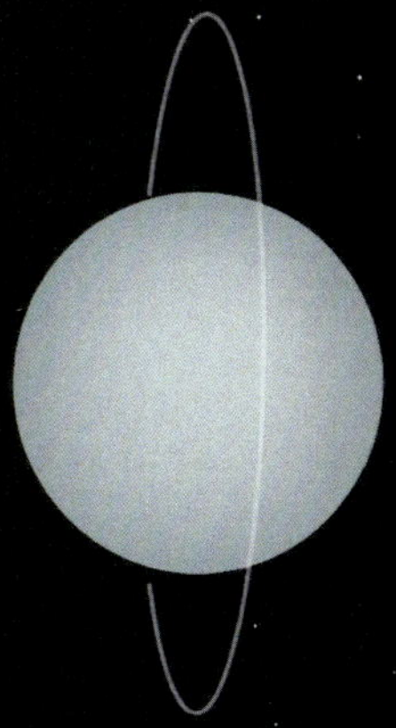

Jupiter is the biggest planet. It's mostly made of gas.

Mars is called the Red Planet because it is covered in red dust.

Saturn has beautiful rings around it made of ice, rock and dust.

Printed By Eyes Wide Digital Ltd, Dorking, Surrey, UK
www.eyeswidedigital.com